The Singer's Collection

Book One: High Voice
Selected & Edited by Alan Ridout

Kevin Mayhew

We hope you enjoy *The Singer's Collection Book 1*.
Further copies of this and the other books in the series are available
from your local music shop.

In case of difficulty, please contact the publisher direct:

The Sales Department
KEVIN MAYHEW LTD
Rattlesden
Bury St Edmunds
Suffolk IP30 0SZ

Phone 0449 737978
Fax 0449 737834

Front Cover: *Boats on the Beach* by Vincent van Gogh (1853-1890).
Reproduced by kind permission of
the Vincent van Gogh Foundation/Van Gogh Museum, Amsterdam.

Cover designed by Juliette Clarke and Graham Johnstone.
Picture Research: Jane Rayson.

First published in Great Britain in 1992 by Kevin Mayhew Ltd.

© Copyright 1992 Kevin Mayhew Ltd.

ISBN 0 86209 270 1

All or part of these pieces have been edited by
Alan Ridout and are the copyright of Kevin Mayhew Ltd.

Series Music Editor: Anthea Smith.

The music in this book is protected by copyright and may not be reproduced in
any way for sale or private use without the consent of the copyright owner.

Printed and bound in Great Britain.

Contents

A brisk young sailor	George Butterworth	6
As ever I saw	Peter Warlock	12
Deep in my heart	Peter Cornelius	27
E'en as a lovely flower	Frank Bridge	8
Hawk and Buckle	Ivor Gurney	44
Loveliest of Trees	George Butterworth	24
Nine of the clock	Ivor Gurney	36
Oh! What beauty here is found	Carl Nielsen	5
Roister Doister	Peter Warlock	20
Slumber Song	Max Reger	15
Summer's Air	Carl Nielsen	42
The apple blossom	Carl Nielsen	32
The Birds	Peter Warlock	30
The lads in their hundreds	George Butterworth	38
Things Lovelier	Gustav Holst	48
Were I the flow'r	Landon Ronald	18

Alan Ridout (b. 1934), who selected and edited the music in this book, is one of England's most prolific composers, producing a steady stream of works in most forms: symphonies, operas, ballet music, chamber music, song cycles and church music.

He studied with Gordon Jacob and Herbert Howells at the Royal College of Music and later with Peter Racine Fricker, Michael Tippet, and the Dutch composer Henk Badings. He has taught at four universities, including Oxford and Cambridge, and for over twenty years was also a Professor at the Royal College of Music.

OH! WHAT BEAUTY

Text: Michael Forster (b. 1946), based on the Danish of M. Rosing
Music: Carl Nielsen (1865 - 1931)

Allegretto

1. Oh! what beauty here is found; trees in leafy shade abound,
   perfume sweet releasing. Hear the songbird on the wing,
   telling of the hope of spring, all our senses pleasing.

2. Best of all, the woodland glade holds our spirits in its shade,
   hearts and minds enthralling. Deep within this world of dreams,
   nothing quite is what it seems; hear its stillness calling!

3. Oh! what beauty here is found, Spring is bursting from the ground,
   darkness is defeated! Signs of hope the world adorn
   in the freshness of the morn; all will be completed.

© Copyright 1992 Kevin Mayhew Ltd.
It is illegal to photocopy music.

A BRISK YOUNG SAILOR

Text: Traditional
Music: George Butterworth (1885 - 1916)

1. A brisk young sailor courted me, he stole away my liberty, he won my heart with a free good will, he's false, I know, but I
2. is an ale house in yonder town, where my love goes and sits him down, he takes another girl on his knee, and don't you think that's a
3. grief to me! I'll tell you why, because she's got more gold than I, her gold will waste and her beauty blast, and she'll become like
4. what a foolish girl was I to give my heart to a sailor boy, a sailor boy although he be, I love him better than

© Copyright 1992 Kevin Mayhew Ltd.
It is illegal to photocopy music.

love him still.
grief to me?
me at last.

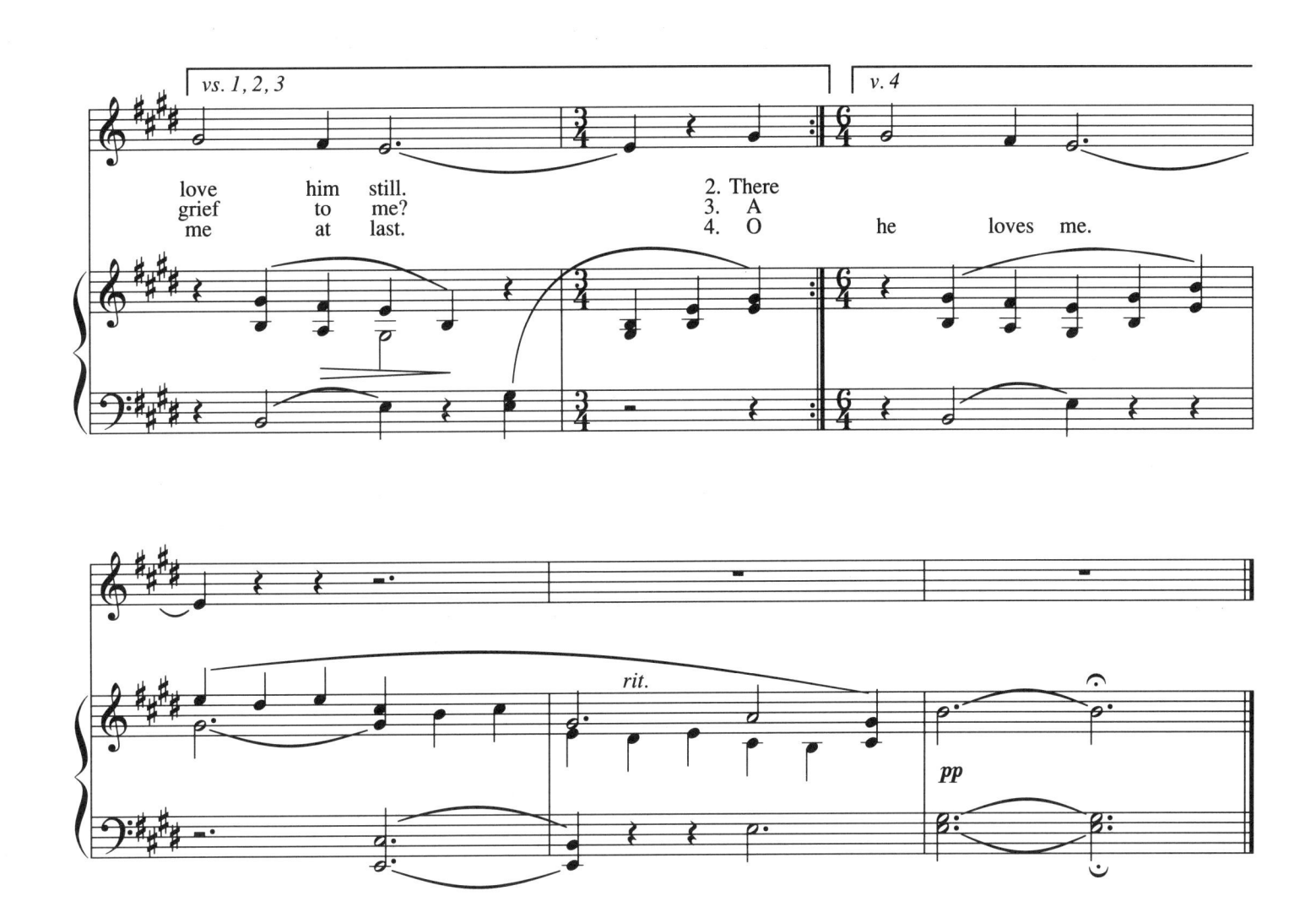

2. There
3. A
4. O he loves me.

rit.

pp

E'EN AS A LOVELY FLOWER

Text: Kate Kroeker
Music: Frank Bridge (1879 - 1941)

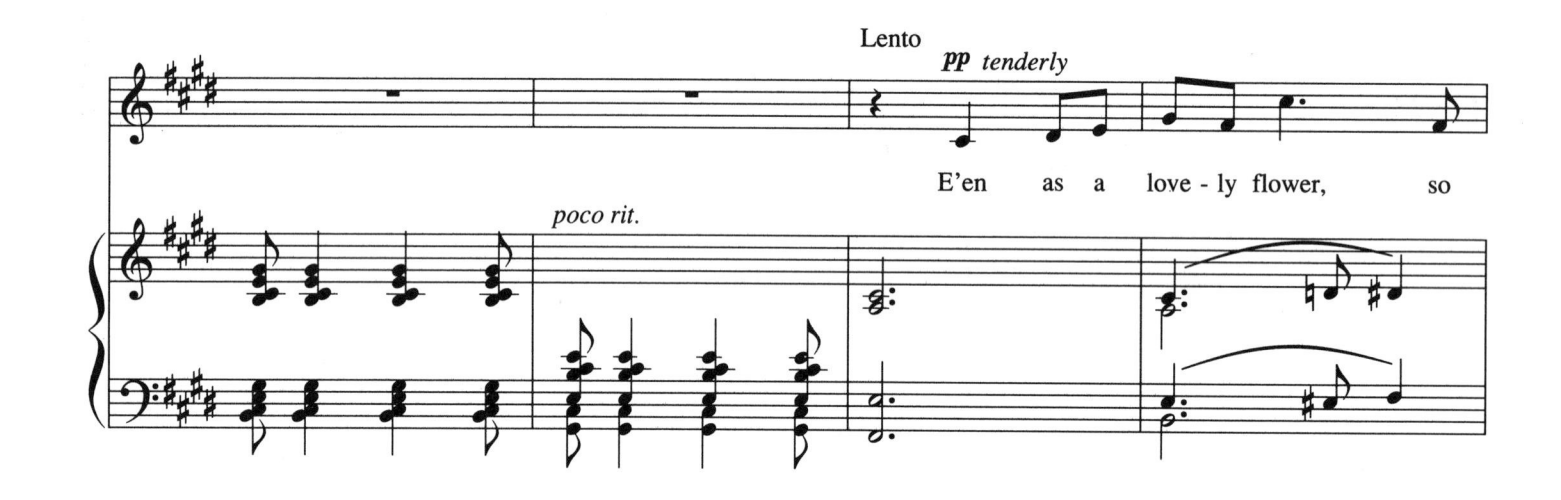

Text: © Copyright Control
Music: © Copyright 1992 Kevin Mayhew Ltd.
It is illegal to photocopy music.

gaze on thee, and sad-ness comes steal - ing, comes steal - ing, comes steal - ing o'er my heart.

My hands I

fain had fold - ed up - on thy soft brown hair, pray - ing that God may keep thee so love -

ly, pure, and fair.

E'en as a love-ly flower, so fair, so pure thou

art.

AS EVER I SAW

Text: Source Unknown
Music: Peter Warlock (1894 - 1930)

Allegro (♩= 92)

She is gen-tle and al-so wise; of all oth-er she bear-eth the prize, that ev-er I saw. To hear her sing, to see her dance!

She will the best her self ad-vance, that ev-er I saw. To see her fin-gers that be so small! In my con-ceit she pass-eth all that ev-er I saw. Na-ture in her hath won-der-ly wrought. Christ ne-ver such an-oth-er bought, that ev-er I saw.

I have seen ma-ny that have beau-ty, yet is there none like to my la-dy that ev-er I saw. There-fore I dare this bold-ly say, I shall have the best and fair-est may that ev-er I saw, that ev-er I saw.

SLUMBER SONG

Text: Michael Forster (b. 1946), based on the German of M. Boeli
Music: Max Reger (1873 - 1916)

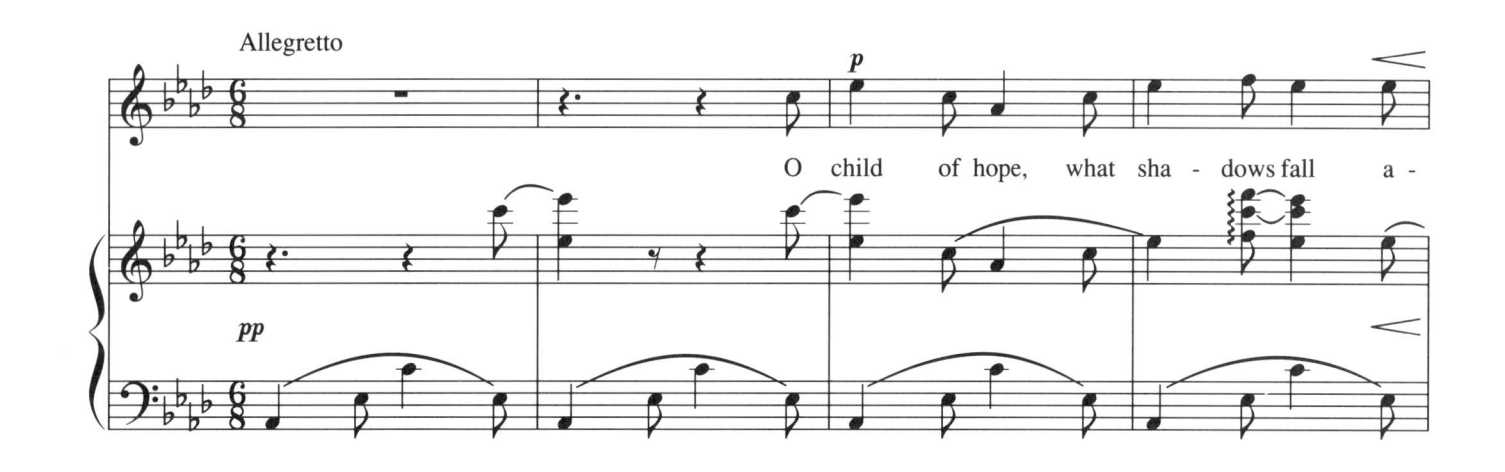

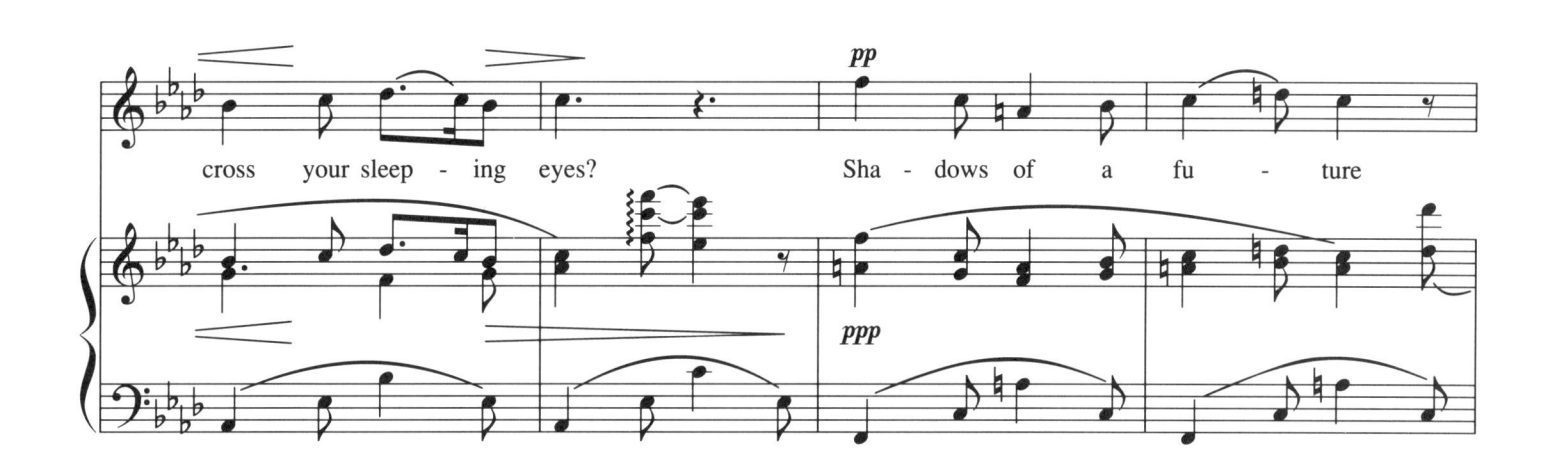

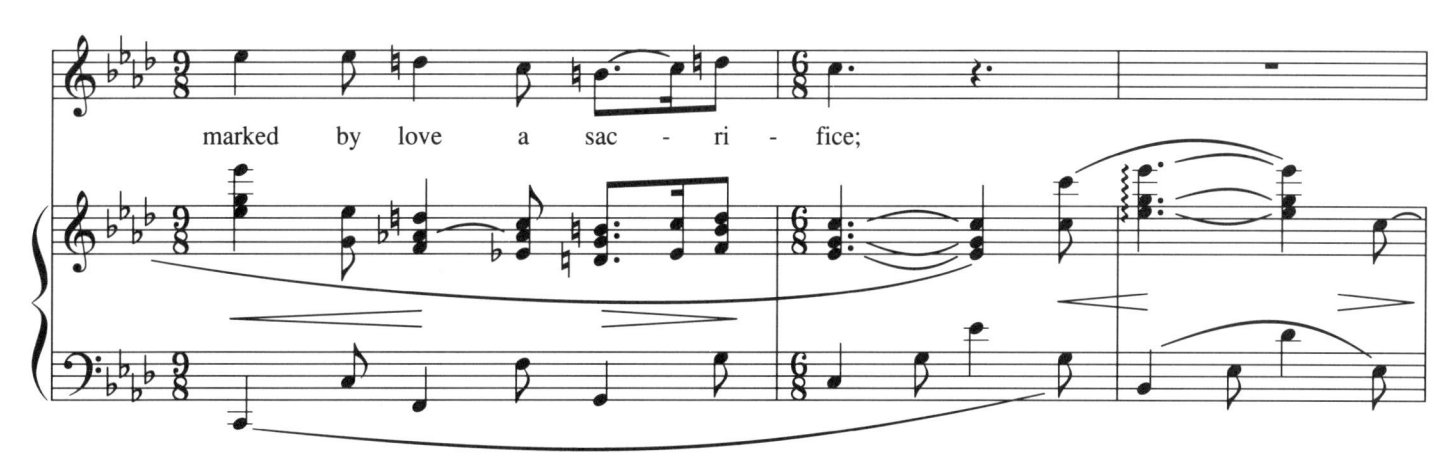

© Copyright 1992 Kevin Mayhew Ltd.
It is illegal to photocopy music.

O child of pro - mise such a cost, but such a prize!

O soft - ly slum - ber, child of grace!

Child of sor - row child of joy child of my - ste -

ry di - vine, may your peace-ful, trust-ing sleep be of hope the seal and sign. O soft-ly slum - ber, child of grace.

WERE I THE FLOW'R

Text: Edward Teschemacher (1909 - 1940)
Music: Landon Ronald (1873 - 1938)

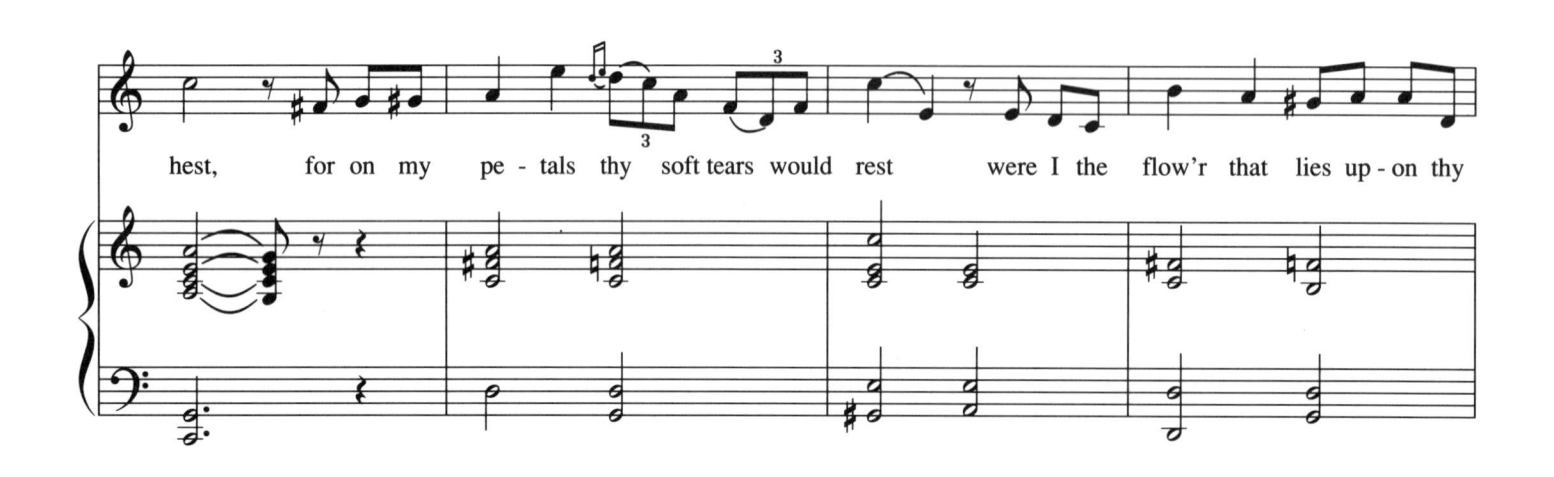

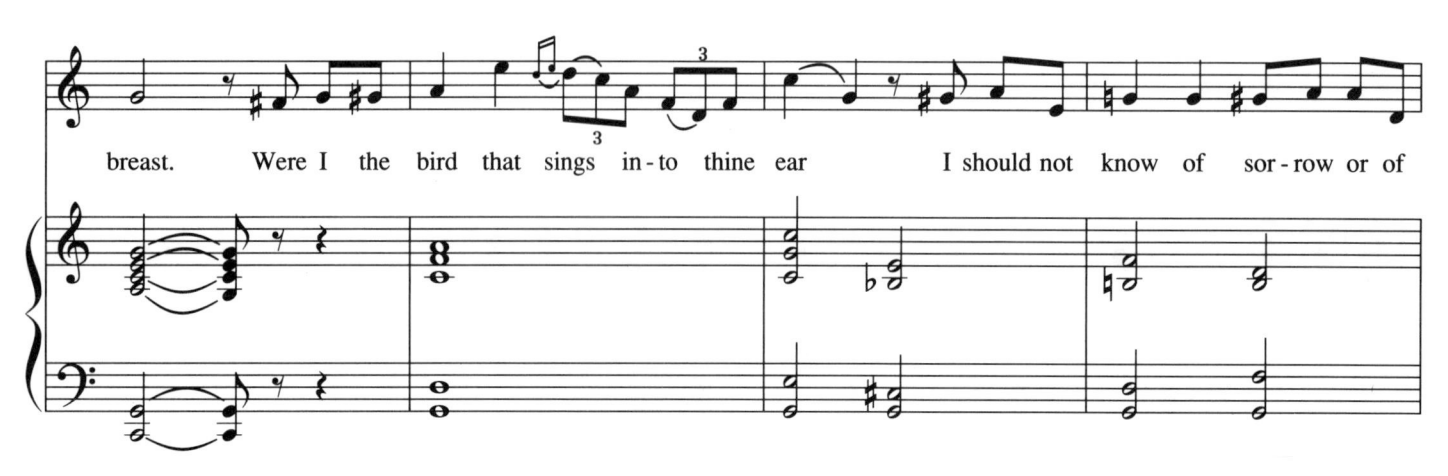

Andante con moto

Were I the flow'r that lies up-on thy breast, I should no lon-ger weep in love's be-hest, for on my pe-tals thy soft tears would rest were I the flow'r that lies up-on thy breast. Were I the bird that sings in-to thine ear I should not know of sor-row or of

© Copyright 1992 Kevin Mayhew Ltd.
It is illegal to photocopy music.

fear, my heart would tell thee all, thy heart would hear were I the bird that sings in-to thine ear. Were I the star that shines up-on thy grave, I should no lon-ger for the cold earth crave, but speed with thee but speed with thee be-yond the win-try wave were I the star that shines up-on thy grave!

ROISTER DOISTER

Text: Nicholas Udall (1505 -,1556)
Music: Peter Warlock (1894 - 1930)

Roisterdoisterously

I mun be mar-ried a Sun - day, I mun be mar-ried a Sun - day, who - so - ev - er shall come that way, I mun be mar-ried a

© Copyright 1992 Kevin Mayhew Ltd.
It is illegal to photocopy music.

Sun - day. Rois - ter Dois - ter is my name, Rois - ter Dois - ter
marcato non legato
is my name, a lus - ty brute I am the same, I mun be mar - ried a
sffz
Sun - day.
p
Christ - ian Cus - tance have I found,
p
Christ - ian Cus - tance have I found, a wid - ow worth a thou - sand pound, I

mun be mar-ried a Sun-day. Cus-tance is as sweet as hon-ey, Cus-tance is as sweet as hon-ey. I her lamb and she my con-ey; I mun be mar-ried a Sun-day. When we shall make our wedd-ing feast, when we shall make our wedd-ing feast, there shall be cheer for man and beast; I mun be mar-ried a Sun - day. I mun be mar-ried a Sun - day, I mun be mar-ried a Sun - day; who - so - ev - er shall come that way, I mun be mar-ried a Sun - day.

LOVELIEST OF TREES

Text: A. E. Housman (1859 - 1936)
Music: George Butterworth (1885 - 1916)

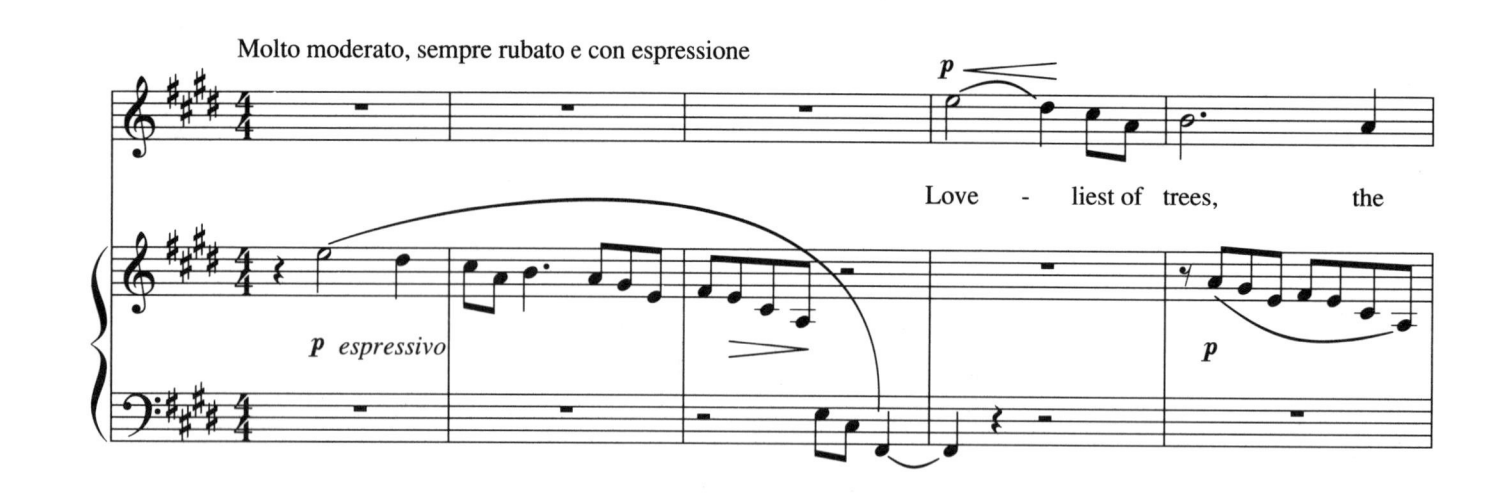

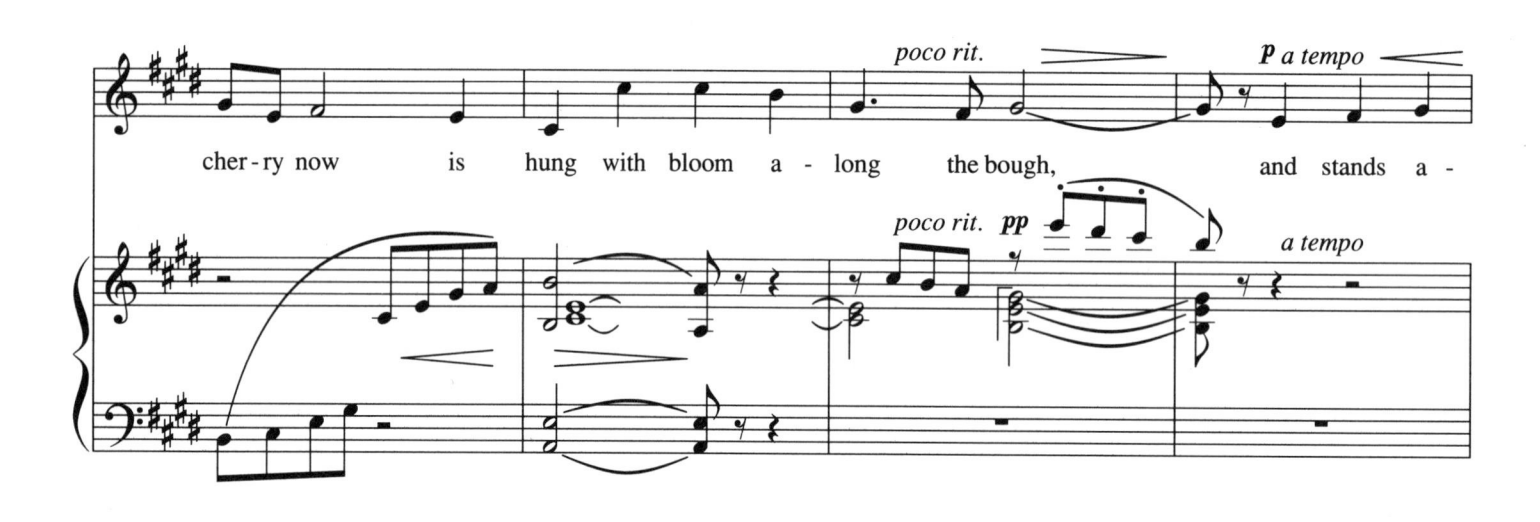

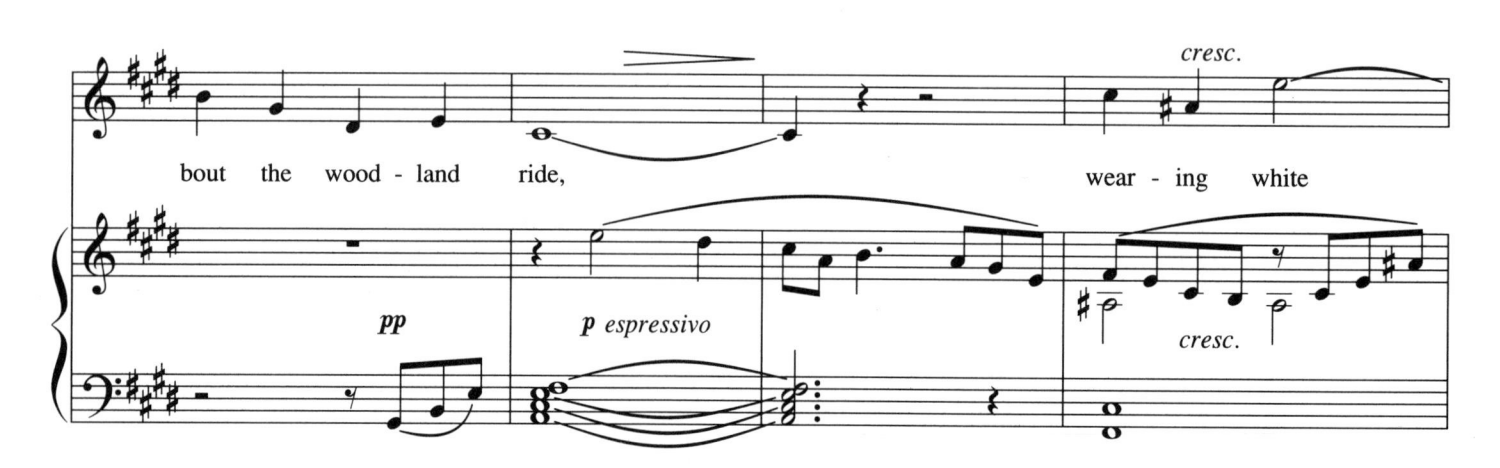

Molto moderato, sempre rubato e con espressione

Love-liest of trees, the cher-ry now is hung with bloom a-long the bough, and stands a-bout the wood-land ride, wear-ing white

© Copyright 1992 Kevin Mayhew Ltd.
It is illegal to photocopy music.

for Eas - ter - tide.

Now, of my three-score years and ten, twen-ty will not come a-gain, and take from seven-ty springs a score, it on-ly leaves me fif-ty more.

And since to look at things in bloom fif-ty springs are lit-tle room, a-bout the wood-lands I will go to see the cher-ry hung with snow.

DEEP IN MY HEART

Text: Michael Forster (b. 1946), based on the German of Peter Cornelius
Music: Peter Cornelius (1824 - 1874)

Andantino

Deep in my heart, my love will flower, it is for you I long, love. You fill my ev-ery wa-king hour, you are my eve-ning song, love. You

© Copyright 1992 Kevin Mayhew Ltd.
It is illegal to photocopy music.

are my eve-ning song, love. I wish you all that's good and gold and trea-sures ever new, love; but best by far, to have and hold, my heart's de-sire is you, love. My food and drink, my ve-ry life, un-

til my dy - ing day, love; my on - ly joy, my love, my wife, come
cresc.
be my own, oh stay, love. My on - ly joy, my love, my wife, come
mf
p
p
be my own, oh stay, love. Oh stay, love.
p

THE BIRDS

Text: Hilaire Belloc (1870 - 1953)
Music: Peter Warlock (1894 - 1930)

Allegretto semplice

When Jesus Christ was four years old, the angels brought him toys of gold, which no man ever had bought or sold. And yet with these he would not play. He made him small fowl out of clay, and

Text: © Copyright Peter Fraser and Dunlop Ltd., 503/4 The Chambers, Lotts Road, Chelsea Harbour, London SW10 OXS.
Reproduced by kind permission.
Music: © Copyright 1992 Kevin Mayhew Ltd.
It is illegal to photocopy music.

blessed them till they flew a - way.

Tu cre - as - ti, Do - mi - ne.

Poco meno mosso

Je - sus Christ, thou child so wise, bless mine hands and fill mine eyes, and

bring my soul to Pa - ra - dise.

THE APPLE BLOSSOM

Text: Michael Forster (b. 1946), based on the Danish of L. Holstein
Music: Carl Nielsen (1865 - 1931)

seem to know the song her dan-cing heart would sing, and tell how all her be-ing longs to be his bride of spring.

A-wak-ened by his morn-ing kiss, she breathes, she breathes through-out the day, and revels in his gol-den ray. And when he goes to take his rest, she sings her love to-wards the west, 'I love you best.' 'I love you best.'

Now, see the pe - tals fall - ing down; the grass will steal her wed - ding gown, her fad - ing trea - sure and her pride! Jea - lous na - ture has de - nied the dy - ing sun his bride!

NINE OF THE CLOCK

Text: John Doyle (1895 - 1985)
Music: Ivor Gurney (1890 - 1937)

Andante con moto

Nine of the clock, oh! wake my la-zy head! your shoes of red mor-oc-co, your silk bed-gown: rouse, rouse, speck-eyed Ma-ry from your high

Text: © Copyright the Trustees of the Robert Graves Copyright Trust.
Reproduced by kind permission of A. P. Watt Ltd., 20 John Street, London WC1N 2DR.
Music: © Copyright 1992 Kevin Mayhew Ltd.
It is illegal to photocopy music.

bed! A yawn, a smile, slee - py star - ey Ma - ry climbs

down. 'Good morn - ing to my bro - thers, good - day to the

sun, ha - loo, ha - loo to the li - ly white sheep that up - the

moun - tain run'.

poco accel.

mp

f

THE LADS IN THEIR HUNDREDS

Text: A. E. Housman (1859 - 1936)
Music: George Butterworth (1885 - 1916)

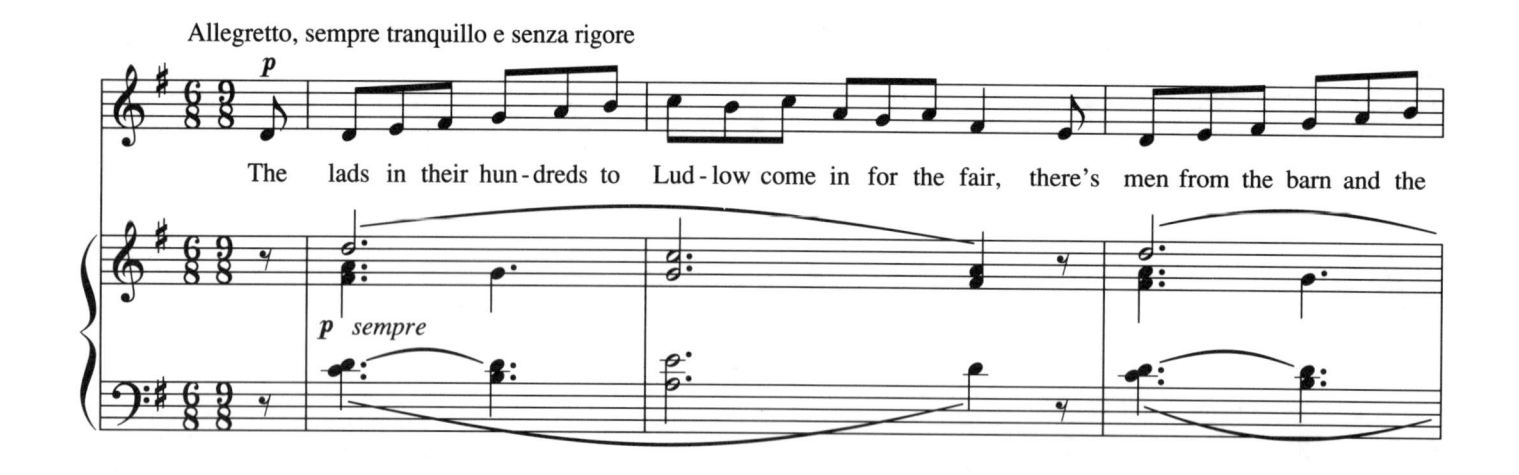

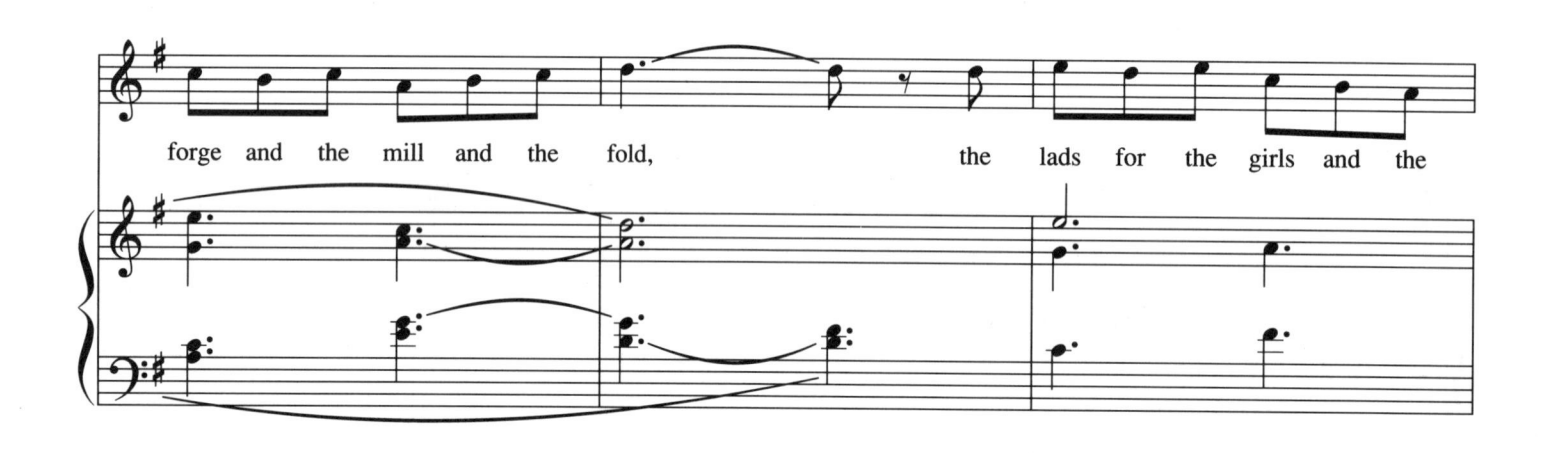

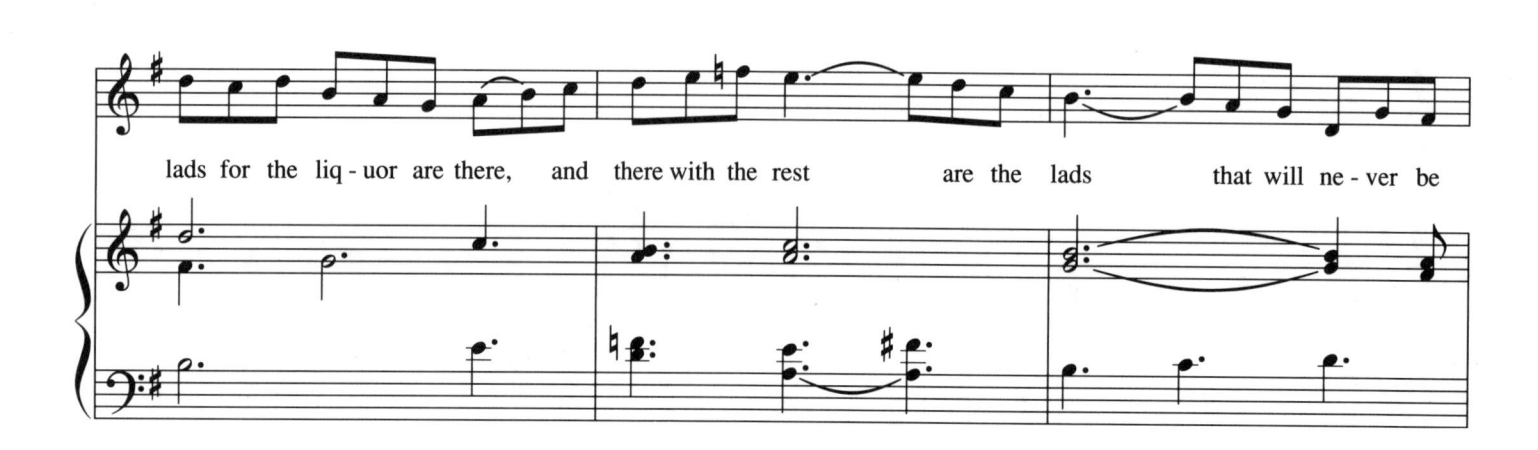

© Copyright 1992 Kevin Mayhew Ltd.
It is illegal to photocopy music.

old. There's chaps from the town and the field and the till and the cart, and many to count are the stalwart, and many the brave, and many the handsome of face and the handsome of heart, and few that will carry their looks or their truth to the grave. I

wish one could know them, I wish there were tok-ens to tell the for-tu-nate fel-lows that now you can ne-ver dis-cern; and then one could talk with them friend-ly and wish them fare-well and watch them de-part on the way that they will not re-turn. But now you may stare as you like and there's no-thing to scan; and brush-ing your el-bow un-guessed at and not to be told they

poco allargando

car-ry back bright to the coi-ner the min-tage of man, the lads that will die in their

colla voce

a tempo

glo - ry and ne-ver be old.
a tempo

rit.

SUMMER'S AIR

Text: Michael Forster (b. 1946), based on the Danish of Jeppe Aakjaer
Music: Carl Nielsen (1865 - 1931)

Andante

1. Summer's air, so fresh and fragrant, scented by a thousand flowers, sets my thoughts in aimless turmoil in these languid evening hours, Do I hear my homeland's call? Have we been too
2. Flaming sun, your dying embers streak with red the evening sky; in your home beyond the mountains, listen to my lonely cry. As the shadows fall and spread, soothe the pain my
3. Now a lovely voice is singing to the music of the lyre; tones to conjure hopes of beauty, and the waking of desire. Still she wafts into the air all the magic
4. Could it be my native language, or the unexpected words? Could it be the haunting echo of my homeland's singing birds? Is their song a sweeter sound, falling on my
5. Yet my song, for all its sadness, is a swiftly passing sigh, carried on the flowing river as my exiled nights pass by. Oh those lovely evening hours, resting on my

© Copyright 1992 Kevin Mayhew Ltd.
It is illegal to photocopy music.

long	a - part?	Will she help my mind in - ter - pret	all the se - crets of my heart?
spi - rit	feels:	Will you help me find the mean - ing	of the things my heart con - ceals?
of	her art.	What, then, is my spi - rit mis - sing;	why this ach - ing in my heart?
long - ing	ears?	No, her mu - sic is more art - ful,	but for - give my fall - ing tears.
na - tive	plain!	Brief - ly, still, the mem'ry haunts me	and in - spires this sad re - frain.

poco rall.

HAWK AND BUCKLE

Text: John Doyle (1895 - 1985)
Music: Ivor Gurney (1890 - 1937)

Allegro

Where is the land-lord of old Hawk and Buck-le, and what of Mas-ter Strad-dler this hot sum-mer wea-ther? He's a-long in the tap-room with

Text: © Copyright the Trustees of the Robert Graves Copyright Trust.
Reproduced by kind permission of A. P. Watt Ltd., 20 John Street, London WC1N 2DR.
Music: © Copyright 1992 Kevin Mayhew Ltd.
It is illegal to photocopy music.

broad cheeks a-chuck-le, and ten bold com-pa-ni-ons all drink-ing to-ge-ther. Where is the ost-ler of old Hawk and Buck-le, and what of Wil-ly Jake-man this hot sum-mer wea-ther? He is rub-bing his eyes with a slow and la-zy knuck - le and wak-ing from his nap on a bank of fresh hea - ther.

Where is the daugh - ter of old Hawk and Buck - le, and what of Mis - tress Jen - ny this hot sum - mer wea - ther? She sits in the par - lour with smell of hon - ey - suck - le, trim - ming her bon - net with new red ost - rich fea - ther.

THINGS LOVELIER

Text: Humbert Wolfe (1886 - 1940)
Music: Gustav Holst (1874 - 1934)

Andante (Tempo Rubato)

You can-not dream things love-li-er than the first love I had of her.

Nor air is an-y as mag-ic sha-ken as her breath in the first kiss ta-ken

and who, in dream-ing, un-der-stands her hands stretched like a blind man's hands?

O-pen, trem-bling, wise they were — you can-not dream things love-li-er.

© Copyright 1992 Kevin Mayhew Ltd.
It is illegal to photocopy music.